The Cornfield Volcano

Audie Lee
Illustrated by Jacqui Grantford

Contents

Chapter 1

Fires Beneath the Ground

Antonio's class was learning about volcanoes. Mr. Juarez showed the class a picture of a volcano. A huge cloud of black smoke rose from the top of a mountain. Dark red rivers of lava ran down its sides. Antonio had seen pictures of volcanoes before, but he had never understood exactly what caused them to erupt. He listened carefully while Mr. Juarez explained.

"Now, this is going to sound unbelievable," said Mr. Juarez, "but if we dug a very deep hole under this school, we'd reach rock that's so hot it has melted."

Mr. Juarez drew a diagram on the board.

"You see," he said, "the crust or surface of the whole Earth is floating on melted rock. This melted rock is called magma."

"How do you spell *magma*?" whispered Antonio's friend, Dominica. She was writing notes.

"It's written on the board," whispered Antonio. "Now shush!"

Antonio listened carefully as Mr. Juarez continued. "Now, this magma can sometimes rise up and break through the rocky crust. It might come up through a crack. What do you think happens when this magma reaches the surface?"

Antonio thought he knew the answer, so he raised his hand.

Mr. Juarez smiled. "Yes, Antonio, what do you think happens?"

"A volcano erupts," said Antonio.

"Nice work!" said Mr. Juarez. "That's exactly what happens! The magma rises through a crack in the Earth, and *kaboom*! It becomes a volcano that blows melted rock, smoke, and ash up into the air. When the melted rock comes through the surface, we call it lava. That's what you see flowing down the sides of volcanoes."

"Hey, Antonio, how do you spell *kaboom*?" whispered Dominica.

Antonio frowned at her, and she smiled. "Only joking!"

"Look out of the window," Mr. Juarez told the class. "What do you see? Dominica, you tell us."

"I see our town, San Juan," said Dominica. "I see houses and the church."

"And what else? What do you see beyond the houses and the church?"

"I see the cornfields, and the river, and the hills."

"Yes, the hills," said Mr. Juarez. "All of those hills were once volcanoes. And the soil of the fields was once lava and ash. Our town is right in the middle of a chain of volcanoes. But so far as we know, the volcanoes are extinct. That means they don't erupt anymore."

Dominica raised her hand. "Mr. Juarez, how do people know that the volcanoes are extinct?"

"Well, we can't be certain," said Mr. Juarez. "But there is no sign of any smoke or lava."

As Antonio walked home after school with Dominica, he couldn't help thinking about the melted rock under the ground.

"What would we do if a volcano began to erupt?" he asked Dominica.

"Run!" she said.

"All of us?"

"All of us!" said Dominica.

"It will never happen," said Antonio. "But if it did happen, I wouldn't run. I'd want to see everything!"

Chapter 2

Birth of a Volcano

Each Saturday, Antonio helped his father work in the cornfields. He couldn't wait until he was old enough to drive one of the tractors.

One Saturday morning, Antonio left home early. He walked toward the fields with his pet goat, Pinto. Pinto liked to graze on the fresh green grass near the fields while Antonio was working.

On the way, Antonio stopped at Dominica's house. "Come walk with me," he suggested. "It's a beautiful day."

"Okay," said Dominica. "I can do my chores when I get back."

They walked along, chatting. Suddenly, Pinto stopped walking. He stood very still.

"Move, Pinto!" said Antonio, but he wouldn't go forward.

"What's wrong with him?" asked Dominica.

"I don't know," said Antonio. Then he heard a strange sound. "Listen!"

There was a hissing noise somewhere up ahead, coming from the cornfield. It was almost like a sound an animal would make. Maybe it was a bobcat. But it was much too loud for a bobcat. Pinto began to bleat.

"There's something strange happening," Antonio said. "Stay here. I'm going to look."

"If you're going, I'm going too!" Dominica replied. "We can tie Pinto to a bush so he's safe here."

Antonio and Dominica crept slowly between tall rows of corn. The hissing sound grew louder with every step.

Suddenly Antonio jumped.

"What's the matter?" asked Dominica.

"Something touched me!" Antonio replied. Then they both pointed.

"Look! Moths!" Dominica exclaimed.

The sky did seem to be full of moths, but they felt warm when they landed on Antonio and Dominica.

"They're not moths," said Antonio. "It's ash! Something is burning."

"There's smoke, too. I can smell it!" Dominica said. "I bet Pinto could, too."

They went forward very slowly until they came to a clearing.

"Look!" Antonio whispered.

They saw a long crack in the ground, and there was smoke above it. The hissing sound was louder than ever. A red light seemed to be glowing. Antonio and Dominica went closer and stared at the sight before them.

Red hot lava was bubbling out of the ground. Then, suddenly, there came a great crash like a thunderclap. The ground began moving and rising up. More and more lava poured out.

"Okay, we're not going to run," said Antonio. "We're going to walk. We're not scared. We know what this is, and we're not scared."

"Are you crazy?" yelled Dominica. "Run!"

Chapter 3

Raising the Alarm

Antonio and Dominica ran back to Pinto and untied him. They raced back to the town. Dominica went to her house to tell her parents.

Back at his house, Antonio found his mother and father still eating breakfast in the kitchen.

"Mom, Dad, there's a volcano! In the cornfield!" he shouted.

"Antonio, calm down," said his father.

"It's true! A volcano is starting in the cornfields! Didn't you hear the sound?"

"We heard thunder," said Antonio's mother.

"Antonio," said his father, "sit down and have a drink of water. You are imagining things."

"Mom, Dad, you have to believe me! Just come and look!"

When the family walked outside, Antonio's mother and father could hear the hissing sound right away. The sky was full of ash that rained down like gray snow. Smoke was rising into the morning sky. There was no need for Antonio to say anything more.

Antonio's father went to the cornfields with some of the other men from the town. When he came back, he looked worried.

"You are right, son," he said. "This must be the start of a volcano."

None of the farmers worked in the fields that day. People stayed in the town, gathering to talk with friends. Would there be a big eruption? What would happen to their crops? What would happen to their houses? No one knew what to expect.

The next morning, everyone woke up suddenly. The ground was trembling. Then there was a roar from the volcano. People ran out of their houses to see what was happening.

Dominica and her family saw Antonio and his family. They hurried toward one another. But before they could say a word, people in the crowd started shouting. "Look! The volcano!" Everyone stopped and stared.

There wasn't just smoke and ash in the sky anymore. The people could see the top of the volcano. Instead of a crack in the ground, now there was a small mountain!

When Antonio's family was back home, they turned on the radio to listen to the news. There was an announcement from the mayor. The state government had been informed of the emergency and help was on its way. But the mayor warned the people of San Juan that they might be forced to leave their homes. If the volcano continued to erupt, it would be too dangerous to stay.

Chapter 4

Leaving San Juan

All that day, the volcano kept growing and growing. By noon, people were beginning to leave the town. Many people were upset, not knowing if they would ever see their homes again. Dominica's family decided to leave for San Bernardo, a town near the coast. They had relatives there.

"I'll miss you," said Dominica, when she came to say goodbye to Antonio. "Please be careful."

"I will," promised Antonio.

As people were leaving San Juan, other people were arriving. Policemen and soldiers were sent by the state government. Reporters and scientists rushed to the town, too. They had heard about the amazing birth of the volcano and wanted to see it for themselves.

Antonio and his parents watched all through the afternoon as the volcano grew taller and taller. The ash was spreading over the cornfields, burying the corn. Red streaks of lava caused fires in the fields. Falling ash put the fires out, but by evening, all the corn plants had been destroyed. The smoke was growing thicker and thicker. The smell of sulfur was so strong that Antonio had to cover his mouth and nose with a cloth.

"We must leave San Juan," Antonio's mother said. "I don't want to leave our home, but it is too dangerous to stay."

Antonio's father agreed. "You're right. We will leave in the morning." He shook his head sadly and thought for a few moments. "I can't believe it," he said. "The whole shape of the land has changed."

By morning, the volcano had grown over one hundred feet. A lake of dark red lava surrounded the base of the volcano.

Antonio's parents did not know if or when the lava would reach San Juan. But they were sure there was no time to waste.

They had to leave many things behind, but they packed as much as they could into their truck and trailer. Pinto rode in the trailer with the kitchen chairs.

Soon they joined the long line of vehicles leaving the town. As they drove away, they could see the volcano spitting sparks and masses of fiery lava into the air.

Chapter 5

The Growing Mountain

The volcano grew taller and wider day by day. People called it a wonder of nature. Scientists came from all over the world to study the San Juan volcano, the newest volcano on Earth.

Antonio and his parents went to San Bernardo, the town where Dominica and her family were staying. They decided to live there. They hoped to start a new farm one day.

Soon Antonio's parents learned that the government was going to help people from San Juan buy new farms. It would take years to make a farm like the one they had left behind, but they were willing to work hard. They were just glad to be safe.

Dominica's family also decided to stay in San Bernardo, and Antonio and Dominica remained close friends. Every week, someone would arrive to interview them about the volcano, since they were the ones who had seen it first. One reporter told them that the volcano had grown to more than a thousand feet high. The lava had spread for ten miles!

"And San Juan?" Dominica asked.
"Is any of our town still there?"

"Only the church," the reporter replied.

Two years after the eruption of the volcano, Antonio and Dominica returned to San Juan with their families. They wanted to see what had happened to the town they had left behind. What they saw amazed them. The volcano rose high into the sky, still belching ash and lava from its top. The streets of San Juan were covered with hardened lava. The cornfields no longer existed.

"The volcano is still growing," said Dominica. "It just keeps erupting."

"But one day it will stop," said Antonio. "The lava will turn into rich soil."

"Yes," said Dominica. "People will have farms here. One day, San Juan will have new cornfields. And families will live here again, with children just like us."

Volcanoes

Under the surface of the Earth, there is hot, melted rock. Sometimes the melted rock bursts through Earth's surface as lava. This is what happens when a volcano erupts.

Most volcanoes are shaped like mountains, but the land may have been flat when the volcano started erupting. As lava and ash from a volcano cool down, they form solid rock. The shape of the land can change as layers of rock build up.

The sides of this volcano are covered with flowing lava.

The Paricutín Volcano

The volcanic eruption described in the story is based on a real event in Mexico. One day in 1943, some farmers saw a long crack suddenly appear in the ground. Smoke and ash poured out of it. Soon lava began to erupt. The farmers and other people in the village were seeing the beginning of a volcanic eruption.

After one day, the lava had formed a mound as big as a house. The eruption continued, and the volcano grew and grew. After a year, the volcano was more than 1,000 feet tall!

This picture shows the volcano and the remains of a nearby town.

Write an Interview

Imagine that you are a newspaper reporter. What questions would you ask in an interview with Antonio or Dominica?

- Copy the chart below.
- Decide who you will interview: Antonio or Dominica.
- In the first column, write questions you will ask in your interview.
- In the second column, write how Dominica or Antonio would respond.

Interview with _____

Questions	Answers

Think About the Story

In *The Cornfield Volcano*, Antonio and Dominica are the first people to see the volcano forming in the cornfield. Think about these questions.

- At school, what do Antonio and Dominica learn about volcanoes?

- What do Antonio and Dominica see when they go out to the fields?

- How is San Juan different when Antonio and Dominica go back two years later?

To learn more about our changing Earth, read the books below.

SUGGESTED READING
Windows on Literacy
Volcanoes
Slow Changes on Earth

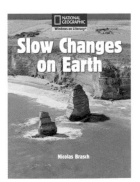